CW01509871

WALKING CLOS

CHELMSFORD

in Essex

Number Fifty in the popular series of walking guides

Contents

Walked, Written and Drawn by Clive Brown
© Clive Brown 2009 – 2019

Published by Clive Brown
ISBN 978-1-907669-50-7

PLEASE
Take care of the countryside
Your leisure is someone's livelihood

Close gates
Start no fires
Keep away from livestock and animals
Do not stray from marked paths
Take litter home
Do not damage walls, hedgerows or fences
Cross only at stiles or gates
Protect plants, trees and wildlife
Keep dogs on leads
Respect crops, machinery and rural property
Do not contaminate water

Although not essential we recommend good walking boots; during hot weather take something to drink on the way. All walks can easily be negotiated by an averagely fit person. The routes have been walked and surveyed by the author, changes can however occur, please follow any signed diversions. Some paths cross fields which are under cultivation. All distances and times are approximate.

The maps give an accurate portrayal of the area, but scale has however been sacrificed in some cases for the sake of clarity and to fit restrictions of page size.

Walking Close To have taken every care in the research and production of this guide but cannot be held responsible for the safety of anyone using them.

During very wet weather, parts of these walks may become impassable through flooding, check before starting out. Stiles and rights of way can get overgrown during the summer; folding secateurs are a useful addition to a walker's rucksack.

Thanks to Angela for help in production of these booklets

Views or comments?
walkingcloseto@yahoo.co.uk

50:A

Walking Close to Chelmsford
in Essex

Evidence has been found in the Chelmsford area of settlements dating from Neolithic and Bronze Age cultures. The town that grew around the fort on the Roman road between London and Colchester was called Ceasaromagus. During Saxon times it became Celmeresfort, under which it is listed in the Domesday Book. The name Chelmsford was in common usage by the time it became the county town of Essex in 1218. It wasn't until 1914 however that the town became a city, when the Diocese of Chelmsford was formed; the cathedral is one of England's smallest.

The source of the River Chelmer is near Debden Green in Essex, it flows past Thaxted and Great Dunmow to Chelmsford where it is joined by the River Can. The River Wid has joined the Can at Writtle just west of the city.

The Chelmer and Blackwater Navigation (walk no 5) was the canalisation of the River Chelmer. It was constructed between 1793 and 1797 and cost £52,000. The 14 mile long route rises 75ft through 12 locks, from the Blackwater Estuary at Heybridge Basin to Chelmsford. The opening of the London to Colchester Railway in 1843 began a long decline in the canal's business until the last commercial journey in 1972. A steady rise in use by the leisure boating sector has however saved the canal from complete closure.

Pleshey Castle (walk no 2) was originally a wooden fortified structure on a mound, built after the Norman Conquest of 1066. By the 12th century it had been substantially extended and rebuilt in stone by the Bohun family. At the end of the 14th century, the castle was owned by Thomas of Woodstock, the youngest son of Edward III, who had married a Bohun heiress. In 1397 he was involved in a plot against his nephew Richard II, who arranged for him to be kidnapped and taken to Calais where he was then murdered. Pleshey fell into disuse and ruin; the last of the stone was taken away for use as building materials in the 17th century.

Thomas Dixon Ridley first brewed beer at Hartford End (walk no 9) in 1842, by the time of his death in 1882 the brewery was well established with a chain of public houses throughout Essex. The company remained in the hands of the Ridley family until 2005, when it was sold to the Greene King empire. Production was rapidly moved to their factory in Bury St Edmunds and the site at Hartford End closed.

We feel that it would be difficult to get lost with the instructions and map in this booklet, but recommend carrying an Ordnance Survey map. The walks are on Explorer Map nos. 175 and 183; Landranger coverage at a smaller scale is on map nos 167 and 177. Roads, geographical features and buildings, not on our map but visible from the walk can be easily identified.

1   Roxwell Brook

7^1/$_2$ Miles   3^3/$_4$ Hours

Find a parking space in Roxwell, no toilets; shop/post office and pub on The Street. Start from the village hall on The Street.

1   Facing away from the hall turn right, up to the junction at the school. Bear left into Stonehill Lane and immediate right, through the kissing gate; take the track left through the field moving away from the road to the stile left of the house.

2   Cross the stile and bear right on the fenced path, go over the driveway and turn right across the footbridge to the signpost. Continue ahead with the hedge to the right over the next footbridge and the stiles/footbridge. Bear left across the stile at the trees and follow the path along the edge of the trees to the road.

3   Turn left for a quarter of a mile to the bridleway signpost and take the track right, through the trees of Cooley Spring. Turn left on the track out of the end of the trees past a signpost and up the field edge with the hedge to the left, turn left after 150yds and right to regain direction with the hedge now right.

4   Cross the footbridge to the right, turn left on the wide track between trees and continue along the driveway to the road. Take the road right/ahead and carry on ahead as the road ends, up the wide track between trees, then the field edge, past Skreens Wood to the left hand end corner. Keep ahead on a wide track again between trees, take this track left and then right at a junction.

5   Follow this more substantial farm road to a marker post turn left along this narrower path between trees all the way to the road. Cross carefully and keep ahead on the right hand field edge with the hedge to the right, continue with the dyke to the right, up to the marker post. Bear right with the dyke still right and bear left, cross the boundary at the hedge gap and turn left to regain direction with the hedge now left.

6   Go through the gap in the next boundary and turn left over this field ahead which may be under cultivation although a path should be well marked within any crop. At the marker post on a slight right turn right along the wide track to the road. Take the road left for two thirds of a mile.

7   Keep ahead as the road swings right, along Stays Lane the narrow grass track between trees and hedges. Continue between fields to the marker post at a farm track and turn left along the left hand field edge for 80yds to a hidden marker post. Turn right, across the field (a track should be visible) and over the footbridge in the hedge gap. Maintain this direction between fields, going left of the trees. Carry on with the hedge to the right, bearing left then right and bear left to a marker post around the next corner.

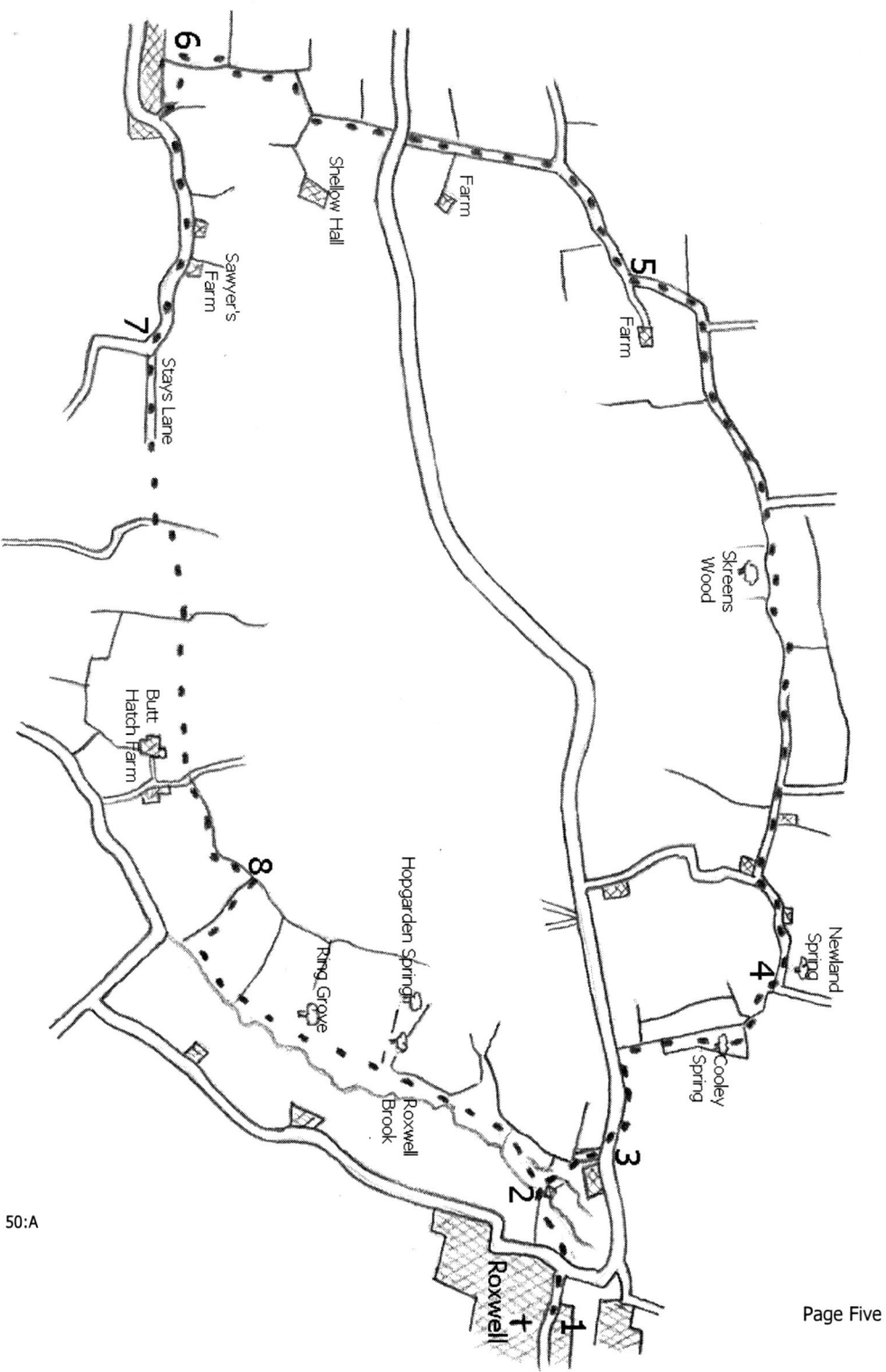

50:A

8   Turn right down the wide field edge with the hedge to the right. At the bottom turn left with Roxwell Brook and the trees to the right, step over the stile and keep direction with the brook still right, over the stile next to the metal gate at the far end. Keep ahead and cross the stile/footbridge at the far left, take a right hand diagonal over this field to the footbridge crossed at the start of the walk and retrace your footsteps back into Roxwell to find your vehicle.

2   Pleshey Castle

6 Miles   2³/₄ Hours

Use the village hall car park on South Street in Great Waltham (open until 6pm), no toilets; shop and pubs in the village.

1   Turn right from the car park entrance down to the T-junction and turn left, carry on past the junction and the 'Beehive' pub. Cross the bridge over the stream to the Essex Way signpost on the left. Turn left along the field edge with the hedge to the right all the way to the road.

2   Cross to the footpath signpost and turn left parallel to the road, bear right and follow the track with the embankment to the right, round to the T-junction of tracks. Turn left on the wider path with the hedge to the right, bear left at the marker post down to the signpost. Turn right with the brook to the left and carry over the footbridge in the boundary, keep ahead to the white topped post in the next corner.

3   Go over the footbridge and return to the original direction with the brook now to the right, continue ahead between the wire fence and the trees to the road.

4   Cross and keep direction on the field edge, turn left upslope and immediate right with the hedge to the left, bearing left all the way round to the road. Cross and carry on with the hedge still left round the other half of Pleshey.

5   At the road, turn left and take the lane right, to the cricket pitch. Turn right around the edge of the pitch to the corner and go past the marker post in the hedge gap. Keep ahead on the concrete farm road to the bridleway signpost at the top of the rise.

6   Turn left along the wide grassy path between trees to the corner of Fitzjohn's Wood, bear left with the trees of the wood to the right and follow this track. Keep direction round the dogleg at Fitzjohn's Farm and carry on along the tack bearing right, to the road.

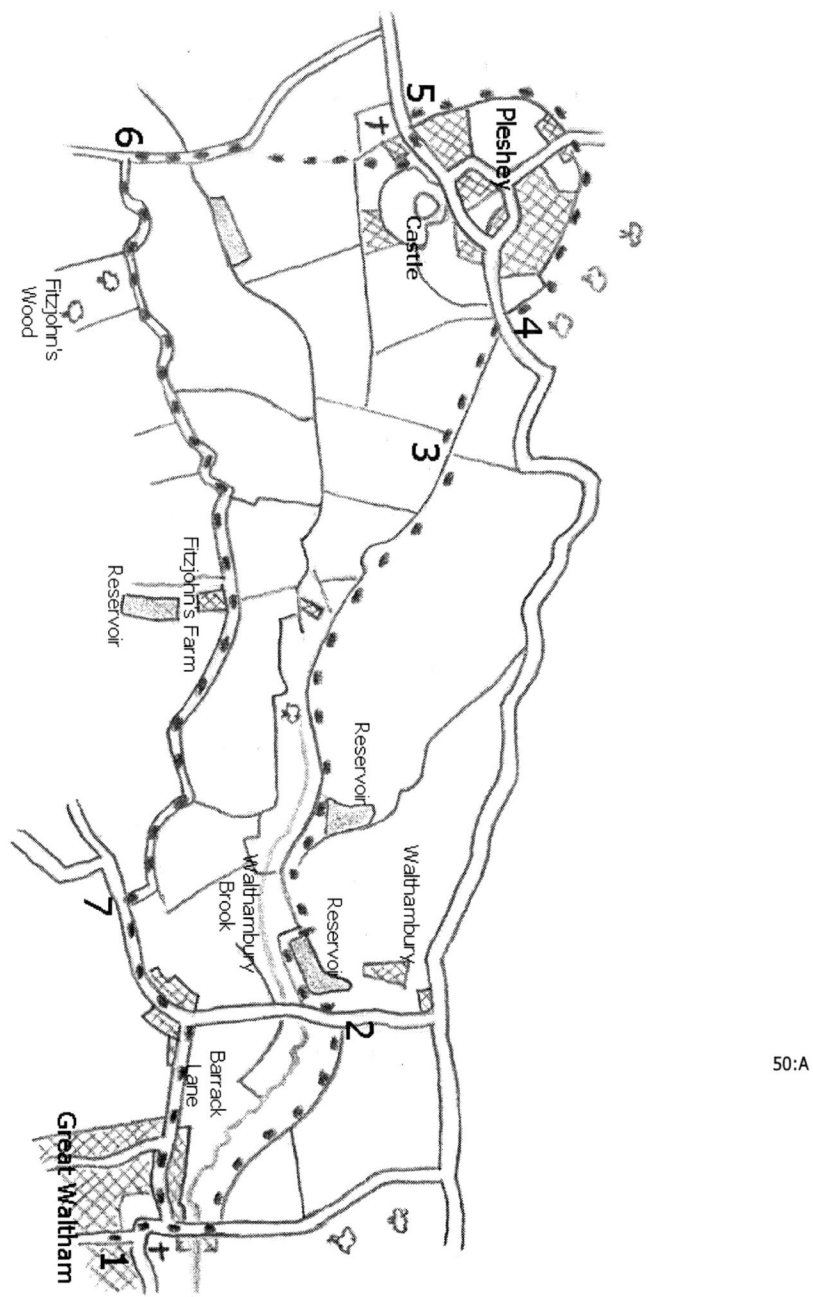

7 Take the road left into Great Waltham and follow the road right into Barrack Lane. At the top turn right and right again into South Street, the car park and your vehicle.

3   Gang Bridge

7¹/₄ Miles   **3¹/₂ Hours**

Find a parking space in Stock; no toilets, all other facilities locally.

1   Start from the church; take the path through the churchyard right of the church and exit through the kissing gate. Carry on between the fence and the hedge, through the trees and up the slope with the wooden fence to the left. Go through the metal kissing gate and keep direction with the metal railings to the left. Keep direction to the road.

2   Turn left and go straight over at the crossroads and carry on bearing left to the main road. Take the roadside path right, to Crondon Park Lane and turn left, follow this road bearing right with Swan Wood to the left, to the signpost on the left. Turn left, through the trees, along the boardwalk and the track with the golf course to the right. Continue to the stile, cross and turn right/straight on up the road, turn right to a footpath signpost and step over the stile (marked St Peters Way).

3   Go down the right hand field edge, cross over the double stile and turn right, with the hedge to the right into the corner and go across the footbridge. Keep ahead on the field edge to the corner and turn left along the path with the River Wid to the right.

4   At the metal girder footbridge called Gang Bridge, cross and bear left/ahead on the field edge with the trees to the left up to the railway. Double back down the steps and go through the unusual tunnel arrangement beneath the farm roads and the railway. Keep direction away from the railway on the path through the middle of the field and continue with the stream to the left all the way to the road.

5   Turn left along the roadside path for a quarter of a mile to the signpost and turn left through the kissing gate. Bear slight right over the stile in the opposite hedge; keep direction on the track across the field, through the wide gap. Follow the path ahead right of the house (Canterburys), up the left hand field edge and over the footbridge. Bear right across this field which may be under cultivation although a path should be well marked, through the wide gap to the road.

6   Cross over the level crossing and bear right past the metal gate, along to the marker post. Take the field edge left with the trees and the reservoir to the left; go over the concrete farm road and keep ahead on the field edge for a further 100yds. Bear slight right (a track should be visible within any crop) to the corner of Spring Wood. Bear left along the edge of the wood, turn right, through the gap as the trees end and then left back to the original direction, down to the River Wid.

7   Take the path right along the edge of the field with the river to the left, all the
Completed on the next Page (Ten)

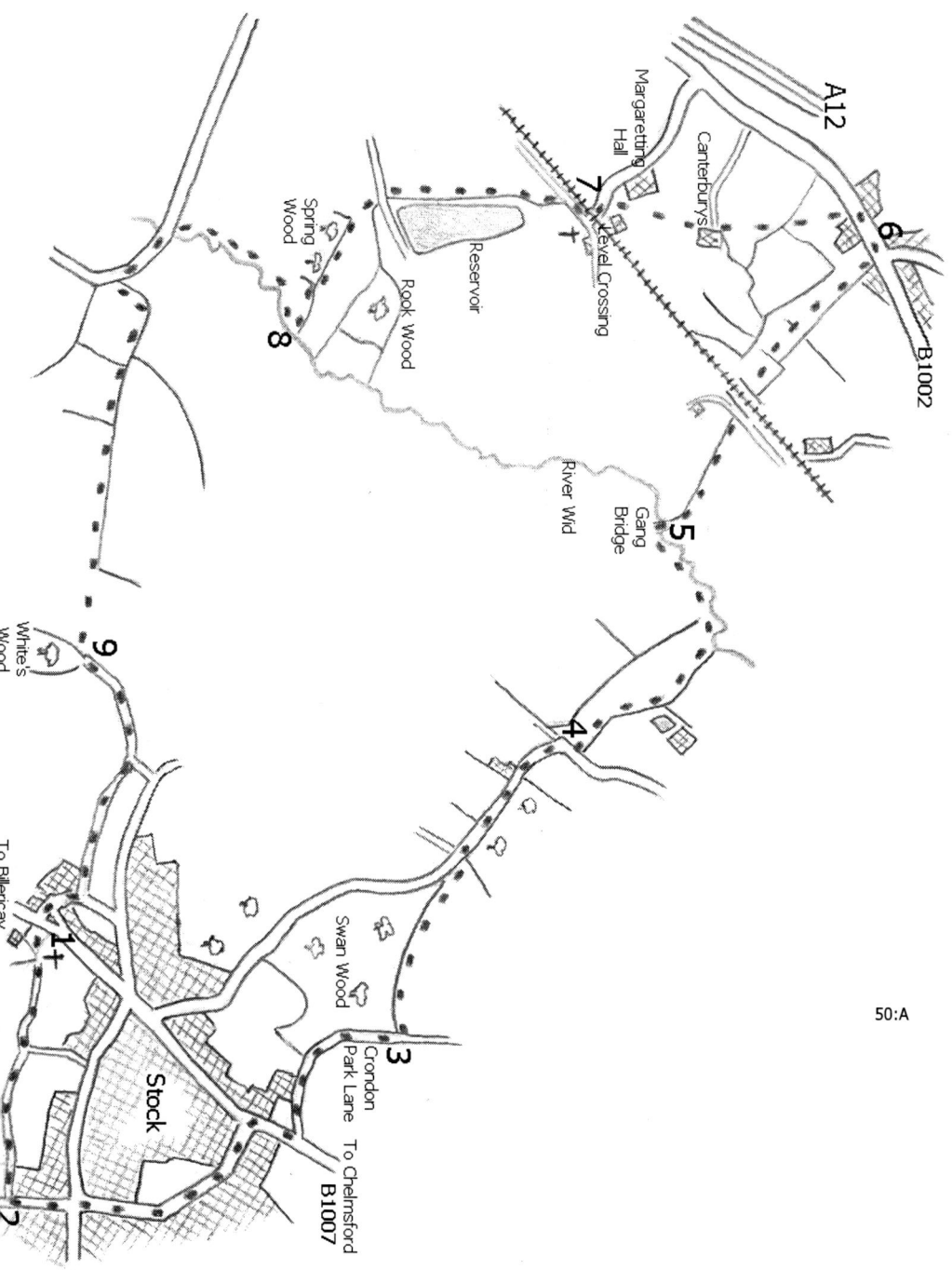

A12

B1002

Margaretting Hall

Canterburys

7

Level Crossing

6

Spring Wood

Reservoir

Rook Wood

8

River Wid

Gang Bridge

5

9

White's Wood

4

To Billericay

1

Swan Wood

3

Stock

Crondon Park Lane

To Chelmsford

B1007

2

50:A

Completion of 3 Gang Bridge from the previous Page

way to the road. Turn left over the bridge and walk down to the corner. Go up the steps at the signpost and follow the field edge left then right. Carry on over the footbridge/stile and upslope to the next boundary; cross the footbridge and keep direction to the marker post at the far corner. Continue ahead across the field (there should be a track within any crop) to the corner of White's Wood.

8   Bear left on the path with the trees right, to the top corner. Go through the gap to the right and turn left up the hedged track, at the marker post bear right, still between hedges up to the stile. Keep direction on the field edge over the stile and along the path between the hedge and the fence, to the narrow road. Turn right and follow this road left to the B1007; the church is close by to the left.

---

4   Sandy Wood

5 Miles $2^1/_2$ Hours

Find a parking space near the village sign at the top of Owl's Hill where it joins The Street in Terling, no toilets. Post office/shop and pub with Thai restaurant.

1   Go along the signposted wide tarmac drive past the village hall and cricket pitch, keep direction through the narrow gate and bear right with the hedge and fence to the right, down to the road.

2   Turn right and continue past two signposts to Gamble's Green, at the next signpost turn left to the corner and turn right. Continue straight on across the field which may be under cultivation although a path should be well marked within any crop. Go through the gap between the houses.

3   Cross the road and carry on slight left along the narrow tarmac road right of the duck pond, past a cottage and over two stiles. Continue up the grass track between fields and follow the path left of Sandy Wood through the boundary and up to the far corner at the marker post.

4   Turn right on the path between the fence and the wood, keep ahead through and over the stile/footbridge. Carry on up the field edge to the marker post and follow the field edge right and left; go through the hedge gap and turn left up the left hand field edge to the road. Turn right for a third of a mile to the signpost.

5   Take the field edge left to the footbridge marked by discs, cross and carry on along the field edge with the trees of Brickhouse Wood to the left. At the end bear right on the path right of the pylon, continue slight left on the path with Hookley Wood to the right. Go through the wide hedge gap to the right and turn left back to the original direction with the dyke and the hedge left. At the far corner turn right, down the field edge to the road.

6 Turn left and follow the road into Fairstead, just past the church turn right and go through the churchyard extension. Turn right over the footbridge and left along the hedged path; keep direction across the narrow field, through the dip and up the other side. Turn right at the hedge, go past the wide gap to the marker post and follow the path left through the wood.

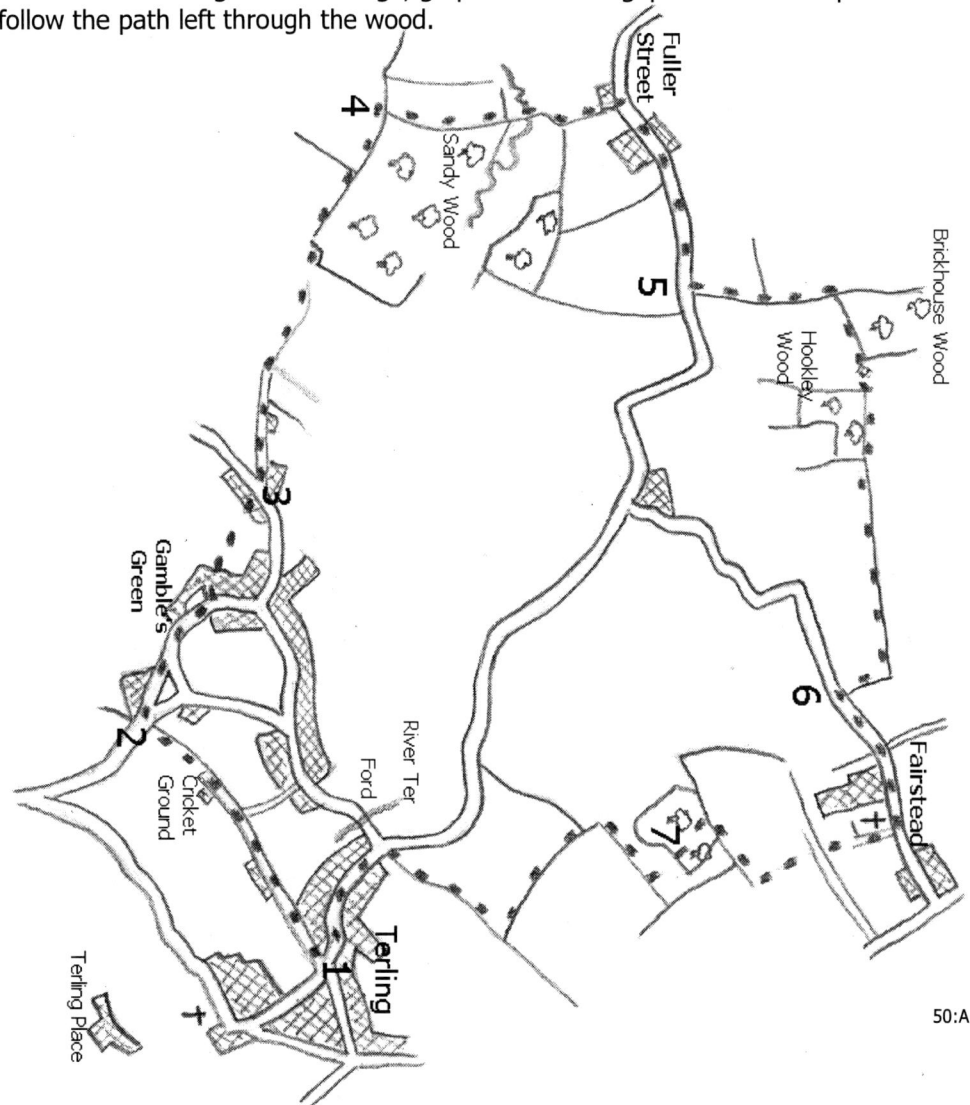

50:A

7 Exit over the footbridge and keep ahead into the dip, turn right with the hedge to the right up to the marker post. Turn left, bearing right, through the hedge gap and turn left upslope on the field edge, hedge to left. At the boundary turn right along the field edge to the road in Terling, turn left back to the village signpost and your vehicle close by.

5   Grace's Walk

Use the small roadside parking area on The Ridge, opposite Runsell Lane, on the boundary between Danbury and Little Baddow. No toilets; there are other facilities further away in Danbury village.

1   Cross the road, carry on along Runsell Lane and turn left into Clark's Farm Road. Keep ahead up the stony footpath and bear left between taller fences. Continue up the path through the trees past the aerial, go through the barrier and the wooden gate marked by a disc. Turn right for 300yds to the marker post at the T-junction.

2   Take the wide path to the left and keep direction on paths and driveways to the road. Turn right and immediate left at the signpost along the winding path through the trees, joining a fenced path up to a white topped marker post. Turn left to a gravel drive and bear right passing close to the left of the white house. Continue past the 'Heather Hills' signboard to a junction and turn right down to the signpost.

3   Turn left along the path between the field and the trees, at the bottom turn right with the fence to the left, into the corner. Take the path left along the field edge and keep ahead right of the house. Follow the paved track to the junction and bear right on this driveway to the road.

4   Keep ahead slight left downslope on the field edge, move slight right down the left hand edge of the next field to the bottom corner. Turn right, with the trees to the left walk down to the River Chelmer. Turn left and follow the path on the river bank all the way to the road at Paper Mill Bridge. Continue past the lock keeping the river to the right for just over a mile to the next metal and concrete road bridge.

9 Miles   4 Hours

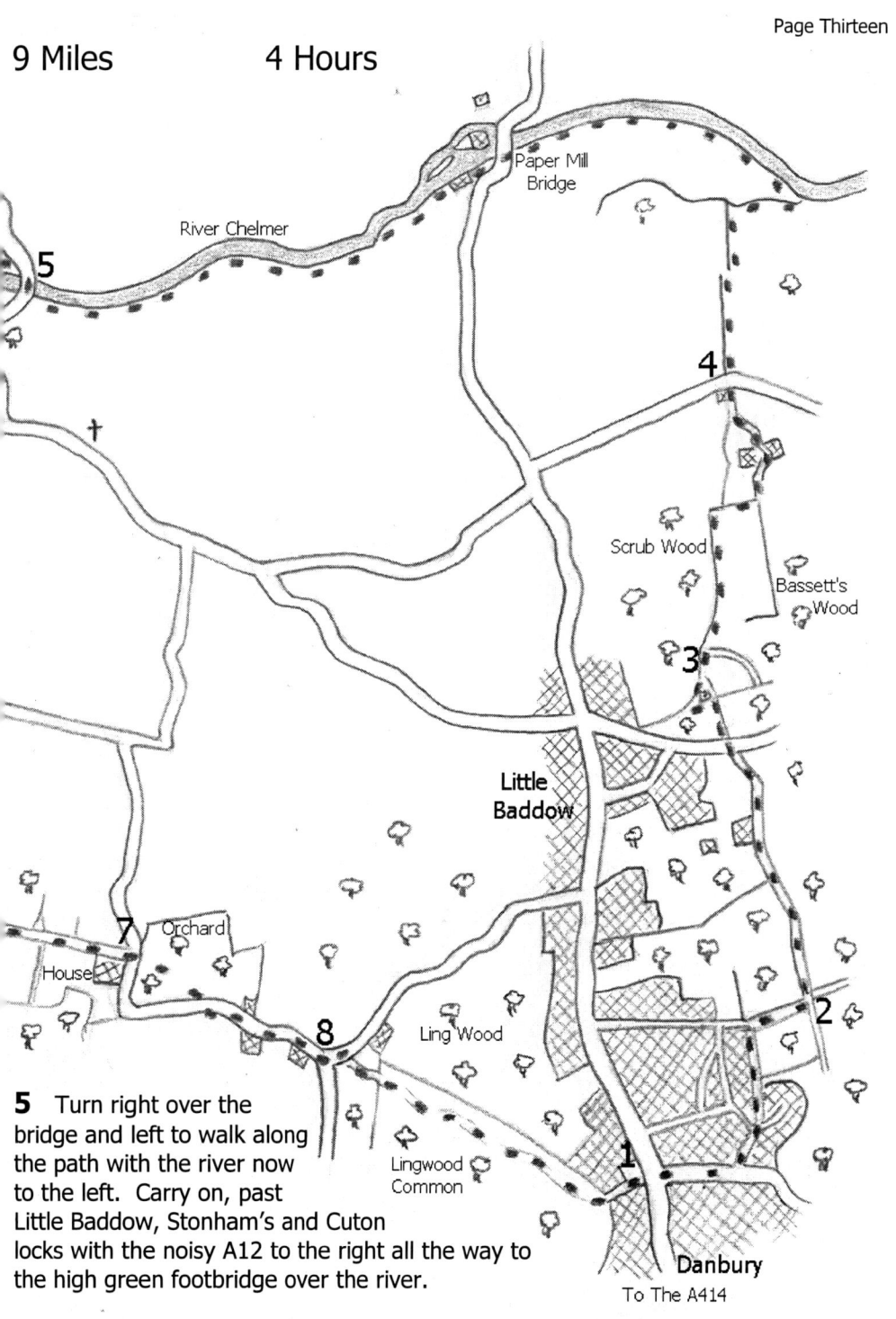

Paper Mill
Bridge

River Chelmer

5

4

Scrub Wood

Bassett's
Wood

3

Little
Baddow

Orchard
7

House

8

Ling Wood

2

5 Turn right over the
bridge and left to walk along
the path with the river now
to the left. Carry on, past
Little Baddow, Stonham's and Cuton
locks with the noisy A12 to the right all the way to
the high green footbridge over the river.

Lingwood
Common

1

Danbury
To The A414

6 Cross and bear slight left away from the river, over the field ahead which may be under cultivation although a path should be well marked. Continue over the footbridge at the white post and keep ahead just left of the pylon (a track should be visible). Cross this surprisingly busy road carefully and continue direction along the farm road, over the concrete bridge and upslope along hedged Grace's Walk.

7 Exit through the gates at the top and step over the stile opposite, turn right with the fence to the right and bear left over the stile. Keep ahead between wire fences through the sorry looking orchard, through the kissing gate on to the road and turn left for 60yds. Cross the stile on the right and take the path parallel to the road. Rejoin the road at the gate, on the original direction up to the junction.

8 Fork left to the signpost and take the path to the right. This path runs a winding course up hill and down all the way through the trees of Lingwood Common to a gap at the back of the car park opposite Runsell Lane and your vehicle.

6   Small Shoes Hill

$5^3/_4$ Miles   3 Hours

Find a parking space in Good Easter; no facilities.

1 Start at the crossroads and take the road towards Mashbury; go through the churchyard and out over the footbridge at the rear. Turn left to the marker post and turn right downslope across the field which may be under cultivation, a path should be well marked within any crop. Continue slight right from the corner with the trees to the left, down to the bottom left.

2 Turn left over the footbridge and carry on ahead with the dyke and the trees to the right. At the end turn left and almost immediate right on the narrow path between hedges to the road; turn right along the road to the signpost on the left.

3 Step over the stile and follow the wide grass track with the hedge to the left all the way to the far left corner. Cross the footbridge marked by a high white topped post and bear right through the grass to a marker post; continue right/straight on with the hedge to the left through the hedge gap at the end. Follow the track through the trees with the River Can and the reservoirs to the right, to the hardcore farm track and turn left up to the corner of the wall.

4 Turn right along this farm road to the far corner and turn right down to the marker post. Follow this farm road with the river to the right, down to the corner ahead. At the marker post turn right up this wide gravelly track with the trees and then an embankment to the right. Continue with the hedge and the trees to the left, past the farm buildings to the T-junction. Turn right, with the pond to the left to the signpost on the left level with the church.

5 Turn left, past the marker post, passing right of the barn and bear right along the wide track between the trees and the fence and the grass avenue between the

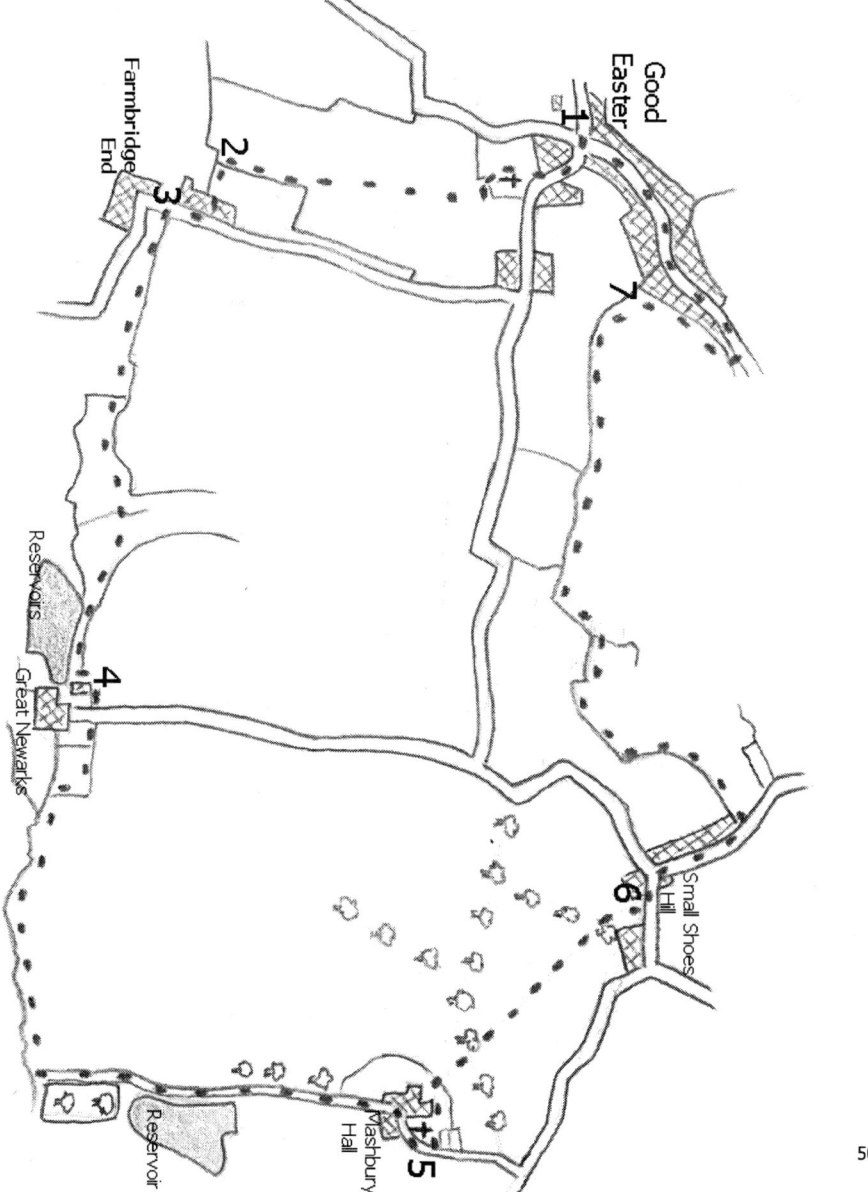

50:A

trees. Go straight on across the massive field ahead (a track should be visible within any crop) turn left up the wide gap through the trees. Turn right along the field edge; go through the gate and on to the road.
<u>Completed on the next Page (Sixteen)</u>

6 Take the road left to the T-junction at Small Shoes Hill and bear right for 380yds to the signpost on the left. Turn left along the left hand field edge with the hedge and the dyke to the left, follow the track left then right and carry on round the dogleg at the edge of the sedge. Keep ahead and cross the wide earth bridge right of the corner; turn left into the corner and right, still on the field edge dyke still left and keep direction to the corner.

7 Follow the path along the backs of the houses, turn left to the road and left again, back to the crossroads at the centre of the village.

7 Queen's Wood

$4^1/_2$ Miles $2^1/_4$ Hours

Find a parking space in Great Leighs; no toilets, pubs 'St Anne's Castle' and the 'Dog and Partridge'.

1 Start from the 'St Anne's Castle'; take the road south towards Chelmsford to the signpost on the left at Victoria House. Turn left past the front of the house and immediate right along the field edge. Continue closer to the road, past the bottom of the steps and bear left with the field edge, the stream to the right.

2 Cross the footbridge and keep ahead through the trees to the signpost close to the fence corner. Turn left, with the fence left to the top corner and step over the stile on the right, carry on along the field edge with the fence and the trees to the right. Cross the stile left of the corner, keep direction and go over the stile ahead; turn immediate left over the adjacent stile. Turn right and continue direction with the fence right, bearing left, through the hedge gap at the signpost.

3 Turn right down the road to the signpost and turn left across the footbridge; cross go up the steps and over the stile. Keep direction across two stiles and step over the stile at the top left of the third field.

4 Cross the road and continue past the green barrier up the grass farm track and keep direction on the grass bridleway between fields. Carry on with the trees to the left and follow the track left under the overhead wires, bear right down to the road.

5 In Fuller Street take the road left for 40yds to the signpost and turn right along the field edge with the trees to the right, all the way to the edge of Queens Wood. Turn left upslope with the wood to the right, through the boundary to the far corner of the wood. Cross the field ahead which may be under cultivation although a path should be well marked within any crop, to the marker post at a slight right, continue ahead up the path between hedges, to the road.

6 Turn left for 200yds to the corner of the low brick wall to the right, take this unmarked track to the right with the large pond to the right. Carry on, through the boundary hedge gap to the corner and turn left between the fence and the black building.

To Chelmsford

A131

Great Leighs

Sewage Works

Farm Building

Farm

Factory

Pond

Queen's Wood

Fuller Street

50:A

Turn right at the sign, black buildings still right and continue through conifers to the road, take the track right parallel to the road, join the road at the 'No Entry' and keep ahead to the main road.

Completed on the next Page (Eighteen)

7   Turn immediate right, the signpost is just a post, past the green barrier and bear left along the backs of the houses. Step over the stile at the shed, go through the gate and over the next stile, carry on between the fence and the hedge. Turn left at the end and walk up to the footbridge.

8   Cross and carry on over the field and the footbridge ahead, go up the slope passing right of the school. Just past the school, turn left along the narrow tarmac path and keep ahead to the road; turn right, back to the pub at the corner.

8   Writtle Park

$5^1/_2$ Miles $2^3/_4$ Hours

Use the car park in Mill Green opposite the 'Cricketers' pub.

1   Leave the car park entrance to the right, past the pub and turn left along Hardings Lane, marked by a disc on a telegraph pole. Walk up to the stile on the left, marked Mill Green Circular Walk and step over. Go down the fenced path into the trees and over the stile, up to the corner of the trees; turn right fro 190yds to the hedge gap on the left.

2   Cross the stile and follow the right hand field edge over the stile at the top right. Go straight on past the signpost, through the trees along the narrow path past marker posts, at the final marker post turn right to a signpost at a tarmac driveway. Turn right and go straight on past a signpost down the driveway, bear right past a metal gate and immediate left along the edge of the trees. cross the stile and follow the right hand field edge with the trees still to the right, over two more stiles.

3   Bear left on a track between fields, past a telegraph pole, keeping to the left hand field edge with the hedge to the left; continue between poplar trees and conifers to the road. Turn right for 320yds to the signpost where the road swings right. Turn left along the hardcore driveway and bear left past the woodclad cottage to the signpost on the left.

4   Turn right, through the trees and turn right at the marker post with the cottage to the right. Follow the track uphill through the trees for three quarters of a mile, as the trees end carry on right/straight on, along the field edge with the trees to the right. Bear right and keep on the farm road all the way to Writtle Park Farm.

5   Pass right, between the barn and the bungalows to the T-junction and turn right, up to the signpost. Take the wide grassy path left for 125yds to the corner and turn left along the track on the right hand field edge with the trees to the right. Continue through the edge of the wood on the track, Chalk Hill, bearing right to the fork in the road at the houses.

6 Turn sharp left on the tarmac road between houses and keep ahead along the field edge with the trees to the left. Go through the wide hedge gap at the boundary and turn right with the dyke and the trees to the right, continue up the gentle slope all the way to the road. Cross and keep direction over the open field, this field may be under cultivation but a path should be well marked, to the marker post at the edge of the wood ahead.

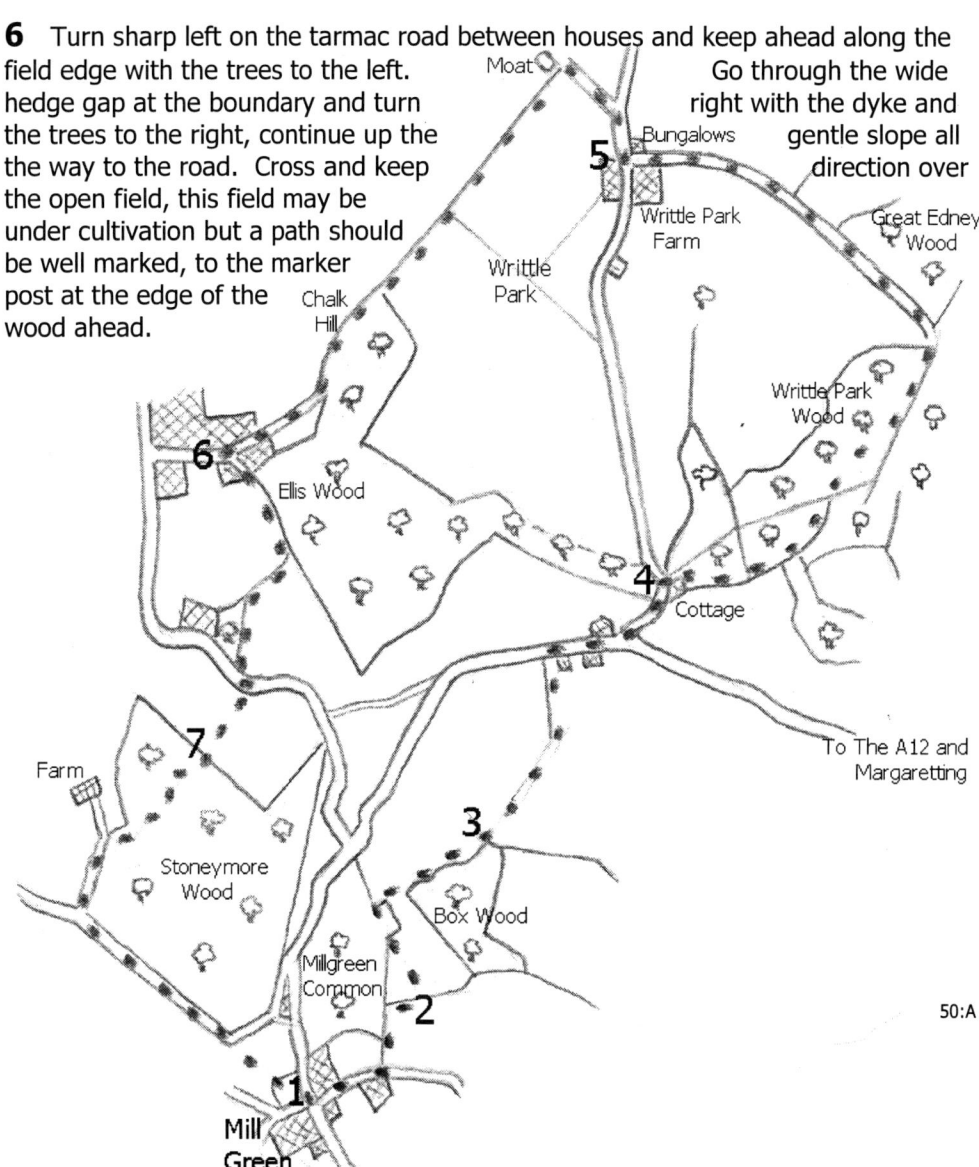

50:A

7 In the trees bear right on a faint track to a marker post and bear left on a still difficult path to follow, to a marker post near the edge and keep ahead to the potholed farm driveway. Turn left down to the junction and follow the main track left. As this track swings left, go straight on past the metal barrier and keep ahead to the car park and your vehicle.

9   Leez Priory

8 Miles   4 Hours

Use the car park opposite the church in Ford End, on the A130 north east of Chelmsford.

1   Turn right from the car park entrance and bear immediate left past the 'No Through Road' sign, along the concrete road passing right of the barns and continue up the wide track with the grassy centre. Bear left, right of the pill box along the left hand field edge to the stile at the corner. Cross and follow the wide hedged track, Meg Lane, to the marker post.

2   Turn left across the narrow stretch of field which may be under cultivation although a path should be well marked and carry on ahead with the tall hedge to the left, into the corner. Go through the wide hedge gap and bear left downslope. Turn right over the bridge across the River Chelmer and walk up to the corner of the mill building. Turn right, through the wooden gate past the front of the mill over the bridge and turn right with the blue railings to the right; keep ahead on the road past the brewery buildings to the road.

3   Turn left and immediate right, signposted Littley Green, follow the road up to the top corner. Maintain direction past the metal barrier, upslope with the trees to the right, all the way to the road just beyond the green metal barrier at the top and take the road right for 800yds to the signpost.

4   Go down the right hand edge of the left hand field to the marker post close to Lodge Lake and turn left. At the marker post turn right, over the footbridge next to the ford and follow the track right and left up slope. Bear right to the T-junction and take the road left up to the farm. Turn left between the barns and right to the road. Walk up the road to the right, to the crossroads.

5   Turn left; go over the bridge to the signpost on the left, turn left along the field edge with the River Ter and the hedge to the left. The path eventually bears left to a marker post, turn right through a hedge gap, past the end of the small reservoir.

6   At the end turn right along the left hand field edge to the marker post and take the wide concrete then grass farm road to the left. As the road swings left, go straight on along the narrow path and turn right on the right hand field edge down to the corner. Turn left with the dyke and the trees to the right; cross the footbridge in the corner and step over the stile. Turn right to the corner and almost immediate left; follow this field edge with the fence to the right, bear right at the end over the stile and on to the road.

Completed on the next Page (Twenty Two)

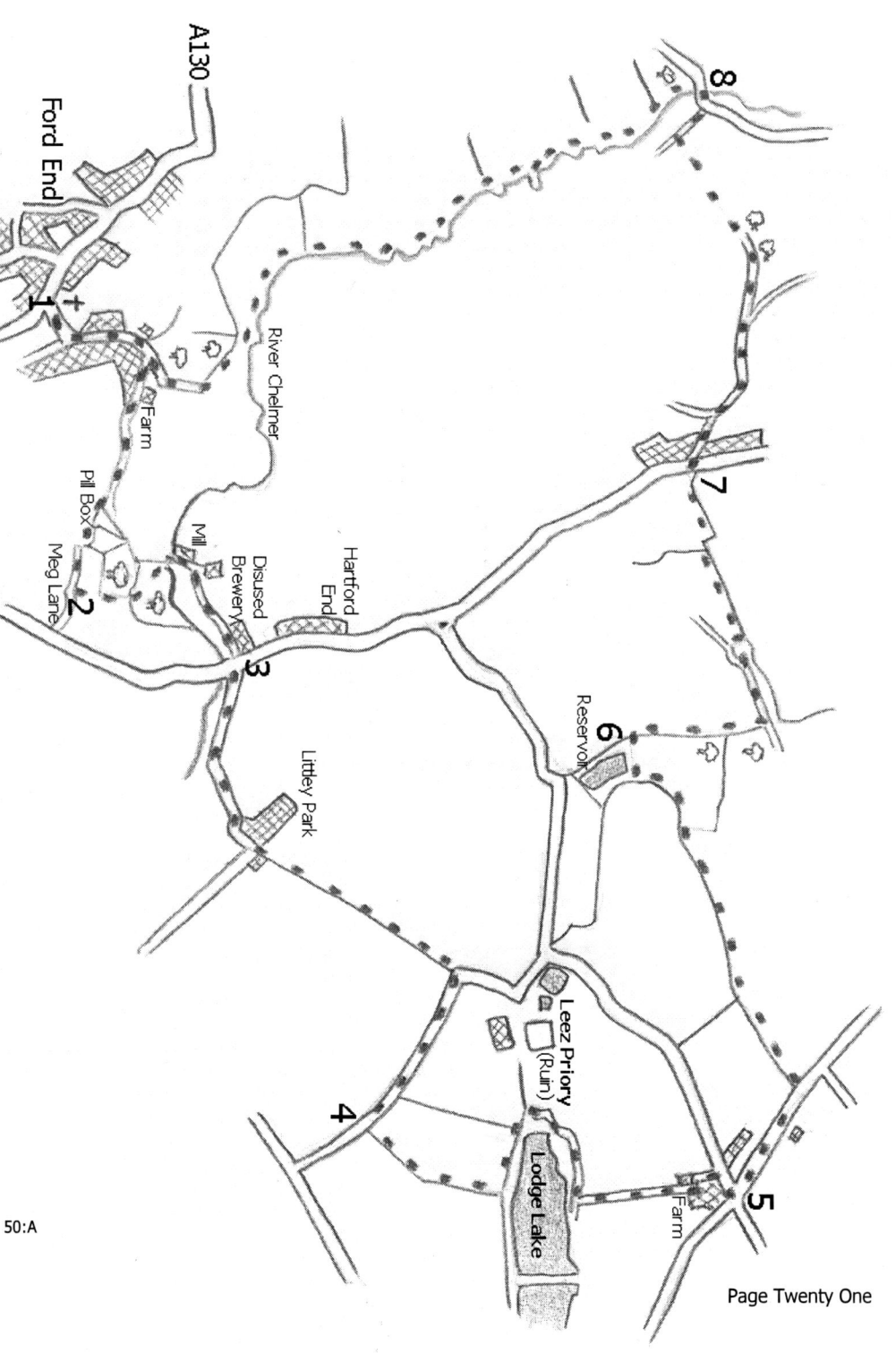

A130

Ford End

1

Farm

River Chelmer

Pill Box

Meg Lane

2

Mill

Disused
Brewery

3

Hartford
End

Littley Park

Reservoir

6

7

Leez Priory
(Ruin)

4

Lodge Lake

Farm

5

8

7   Cross and continue straight on between hedges to the field, bear right and go straight on past the marker post still between hedges. At the end bear left on the winding grass track between fields. Pass left of the grove of trees and carry straight on down a path which should be well marked within any crop. In the dip turn right, down to the road and turn left over the bridge back across the River Chelmer.

8   At the signpost turn left down the path through the trees and continue with the river to the left for a mile and a quarter to the wood. Turn left then right along the edge of the wood with the trees to the right (there is a parallel path running through the wood). At the signpost turn right, along this edge of the trees (look out for the derelict threshing machine on the left) all the way back to the barn passed at the beginning of the walk. Bear right and retrace the outward route back to the car park and your vehicle.

10   Hanningfield Reservoir

9 Miles $4^1/_2$ Hours

Use the car park at the visitor centre off Hawkswood Road on the south side of the reservoir, east of the causeway. Toilets, shop and refreshments on site.

1   Turn left out of the car park entrance along the grass verge of this surprisingly busy road for 475yds to the footpath signpost on the right. Take the track right, between the fence and the trees and bear left with the field edge to the top corner. Turn right with the trees still right and keep direction through the corner at the stile ahead. Carry on through the trees to the road.

2   Take the road left, past the pond; bear right up the narrow concrete path past the signpost and the wide metal gate. Go down the left hand field edge, over a stile next to a metal gate and turn left around the edge of the field to the corner opposite. Continue down to the bottom left corner, step over the stile and carry on uphill, across the stile and on to the road near the church.

3   Go downslope to the right, along the wide grass verge to the signpost on the right and turn right, along the bridleway. Bear right on this hardcore and gravel road, past houses and follow the road left at the corner, carry on for 450yds to an unmarked gate. Go through and take a right hand diagonal, right of the pond, to the far corner of this field, cross the stile and go up the driveway to the road.

50:A

Completed on the next Page (Twenty Four)

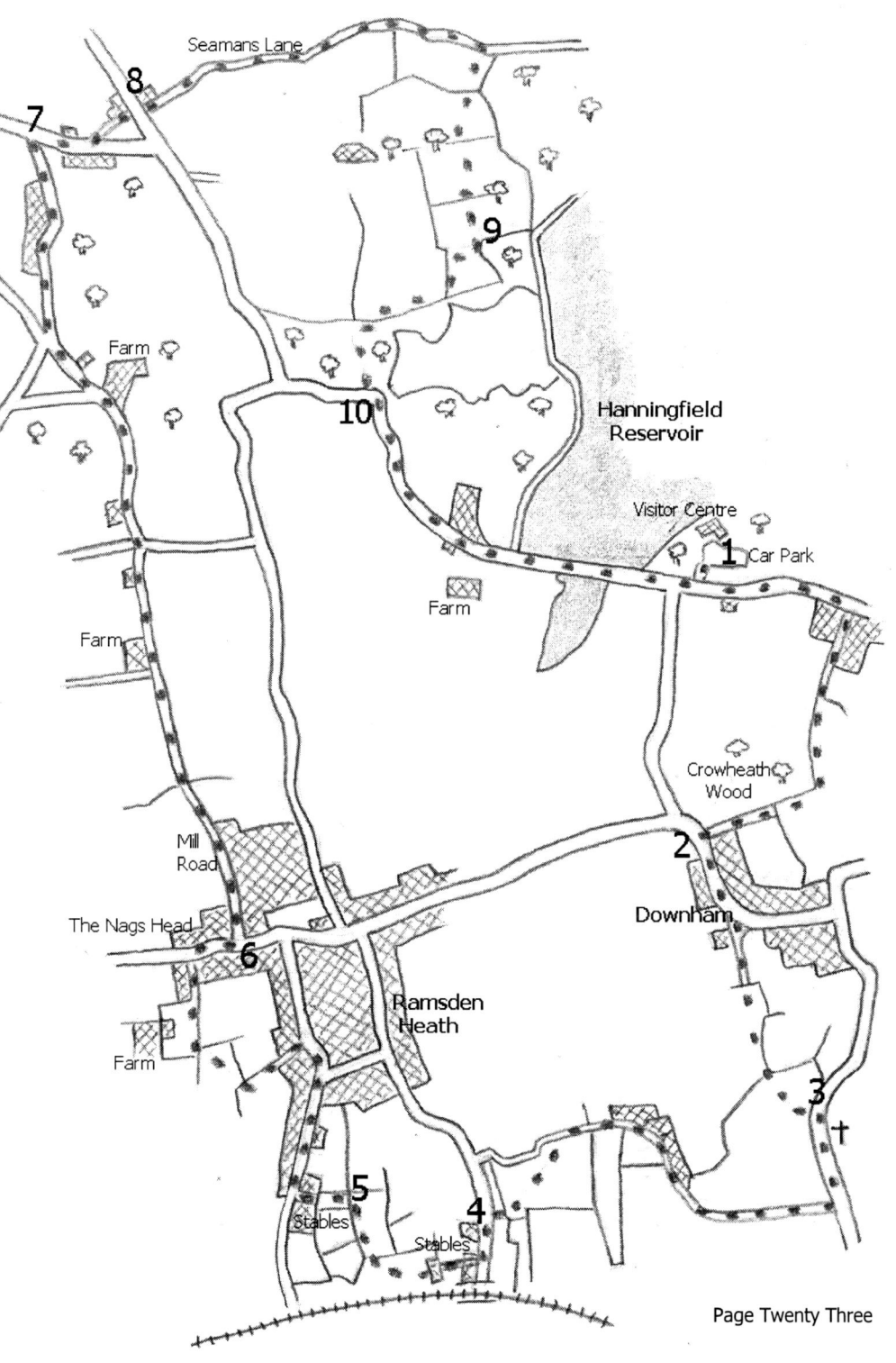

Seamans Lane

7

8

9

10

Hanningfield
Reservoir

Farm

Visitor Centre

1 Car Park

Farm

Farm

Crowheath
Wood

Mill
Road

2

The Nags Head

6

Downham

Farm

Ramsden
Heath

3

5

4

Stables

Stables

Completion of **10** Hanningfield Reservoir from the previous Page

4 Turn left for 190yds to the signpost (which cannot be seen until passed) and turn right (signed Chase Bungalow). Go through the wide metal gate and bear right through the narrow wooden gate at the signpost. Keep direction through a series of kissing gates to the far corner, step over the stile and take the left hand edge of the field ahead to the stile on the left.

5 Cross and carry on along the road past the stables, turn right along the tarmac driveway past the junction with Short Lane to the signpost on the left. Turn left up the driveway; keep direction right of the fence and cross the stile at the end. Bear left over the stile at the far corner and turn left and immediate right over another stile. Carry on up the right hand field edge with the hedge and the trees to the right, keep ahead to the road at the Nags Head and turn right up to Mill Lane.

6 Take Mill Lane to the left and keep ahead on this road/bridleway for two thirds of a mile to the road at a corner. Continue straight on past a junction to a staggered crossroads and turn right; take this road for 800yds to the T-junction.

7 Walk along the wide grass verge of the road to the right for 275yds to the signpost on the left. Bear left between the dyke and the hedge and carry on between fences to a road.

8 Keep straight on up Seamans Lane, the narrow tarmac track between trees. After just over a mile turn right through the wide gap next to the stile, along the wide field edge with the trees to the left. Continue through the wide gap ahead and bear right across the field on a path which should be visible within any crop; go through this hedge gap and bear left over the field and cross the footbridge in the hedge gap ahead. Turn right, to the marker post and left across the field to the corner (a track should be visible).

9 Carry on to the marker post and turn right to the marker post at the hedge opposite. Take the field edge left, with the hedge to the right, turn right, across the footbridge and maintain direction along the field edge with the trees to the left. After 400yds turn left through an unmarked hedge gap and immediate right for 110yds. Turn left and keep straight on along the narrower path following its winding course through the woodland and over a footbridge. Carry on to the road, exiting via the narrow path right of the gate.

10 Turn left and carefully follow the grass verges of this busy road back over the causeway to the car park at the visitor centre.

The reservoir was completed in 1957 at a cost of £6m; it holds 27 billion litres of water piped in from the Blackwater and Chelmer Rivers. The water is supplied, not to Chelmsford but Southern Essex and the towns of Southend, Thurrock, Barking and Dagenham.

50: